# POCKET
# EXTREME TRAINS

A catalogue record for this book is available from the British Library

ISBN 978 1 78521 672 5

Library of Congress control no. 2019942927

Design by Richard Parsons and James Robertson

Published by Haynes Publishing,
Sparkford, Yeovil, Somerset BA22 7JJ, UK
Tel: 01963 440635
Int. tel: +44 1963 440635
Website: www.haynes.com

Haynes North America Inc.,
859 Lawrence Drive, Newbury Park,
California 91320, USA

Printed in Malaysia

Front cover: The Ariel Atom 500.
Opposite: The Ferrari FXX-K EVO.

Photographs supplied by the individual car manufacturers.
Additional images published with the permission of Getty: pp29, 41,
42, 50, 93, 94, 124.

## The Author

Steve Rendle is an experienced author and editor, who has written over 15 books
about cars. He has a passion for F1, and if he could have any car in the world it would
be a McLaren Senna.

# POCKET MANUAL
# EXTREME CARS

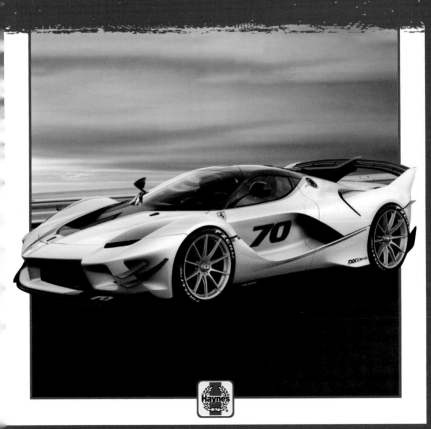

# CONTENTS

# INTRODUCTION

This book is about extreme cars, and we've picked 30 of the most extreme ones in the world. You might wonder what made us select some but not others. Well, for a start, all the cars in this book have been, or will be, available to buy, so long as buyers have enough money, and in some cases if they meet the conditions that the car manufacturer sets. You won't see these cars every day – and there are some that you will probably never see – but they are all out there on the world's roads or tracks somewhere!

Most of the cars are very modern. In fact, a few are so new that they were not yet on sale when this book went to print. There are a few older cars, too. However old they are, though, all the cars included have been selected because they are built to provide an incredible experience for the driver – but not necessarily for passengers… In most cases, the cars need a skilled driver to make the most of them. Some are racing cars for the road, while others are road cars that were built so that they could also be raced.

Every one of the cars included has extreme performance – either top speed or acceleration – and most are able to corner like racing cars. Of course, they all sound incredible, too. Some have road-car luxuries, such as leather trim, in-car entertainment, air conditioning and satnav, while others have no comforts at all – not even a roof or body panels!

Enjoy dreaming, and perhaps one day you might be lucky enough to get behind the wheel of one of the ultimate machines featured in the following pages, and find out just how exciting they can be!

# ABBREVIATIONS AND THEIR MEANINGS

| | | | |
|---|---|---|---|
| **bhp** | brake horsepower – available power of an engine | **Nm** | newton metre – unit of torque |
| **cc** | cubic centimetres – volume of engine cylinders,added together | **rpm** | revolutions per minute – the number of turns in one minute |
| **in** | inches – used for wheel sizes | **s** | seconds – unit of time |
| **kg** | kilograms – unit of weight | **V6** | V-shaped engine with six cylinders (three on each side of the 'V') |
| **kph** | kilometres per hour – unit of speed | **V8** | V-shaped engine with eight cylinders (four on each side of the 'V') |
| **kW** | kilowatts – unit of power | | |
| **lb ft** | pound foot – unit of torque | | |
| **LCD** | liquid-crystal display, eg a flat screen | **V12** | V-shaped engine with 12 cylinders (six on each side of the 'V') |
| **Mm** | millimetres – unit of length | **W16** | W-shaped engine with 16 cylinders (four on each arm of the 'W') |
| **mph** | miles per hour – unit of speed | | |

# ALL ABOUT TYRES

Tyres have codes that explain their sizes, and these codes are usually printed on the edge of each tyre. As an example, a tyre might have a code like **205/50 R15**.

| | |
|---|---|
| **205** | means that the tyre is 205mm wide. |
| **50** | means that the 'profile' (thickness, or height) of the tyre is 50 per cent of its width. The smaller the number, the thinner the tyre. |
| **R** | means that the tyre is a 'radial'-type tyre – it is made from layers of material that run in layers at right angles to the direction in which the tyre rolls. |
| **15** | means that the tyre is designed to fit on a 15in-diameter wheel. |

# ARIEL ATOM 500

Huge power in a stripped-down two-seater for a true racing-car ride

- ➤ Only 25 Atom 500s have been built, all made specially to order for their owners.
- ➤ The car's gearbox allows full-throttle gear changes for incredible acceleration.
- ➤ Adjustable traction control and launch control systems are fitted.
- ➤ The car has an LCD instrument panel that includes a gearshift light.

The two-seater Ariel Atom first appeared in 2000, and is built by the same company that builds Ariel motorcycles. Most models have been built with Honda engines, either normally aspirated, supercharged or turbocharged. All Atoms are super-fast, but in 2010 Ariel decided to build a model with a 500bhp V8 engine, giving crazy performance!

The Atom looks more like a racing car than a road car, with an exposed tubular-steel chassis. The only body panels are the floor, nose, engine cover, and small mudguards over the wheels – if it rains, the driver needs a waterproof suit. A helmet is essential in any weather. The Atom 500, with its V8 engine, can be recognised from its big racing-car style rear wing, and the small pods on the sides of the chassis housing the cooling radiators. The V8 engine was originally built by joining two Suzuki motorcycle engines together, though the final version was built specially for the Atom 500. Driving an Atom is more like riding a motorcycle than driving a car.

# STATISTICS ARIEL ATOM 500

| | |
|---|---|
| Price (new) | £150,000 |
| Max speed | 170mph (274kph) |
| 0–62mph (0–100kph) | 2.3s |
| Engine type | V8 32-valve, normally aspirated |
| Engine capacity | 3,000cc |
| Max power | 500bhp (373kW) at 10,600rpm |
| Max torque | 385Nm (284lb ft) at 7,750rpm |
| Transmission | 6-speed sequential gearbox, limited-slip differential |
| Suspension | Double wishbones front and rear with adjustable pushrod-operated spring/damper units |
| Wheels and tyres | 15in front wheels; 16in rear wheels; 205/50 R15 front tyres; 245/45 R16 rear tyres |
| Kerb weight | 550kg |
| Length | 3,696mm |
| Width | 1,849mm |
| Height | 1,194mm |
| Year introduced | 2010 |

A BUGATTI VEYRON IS HEAVIER THAN THREE ATOM 500S!

# ASTON MARTIN ONE-77

Aston Martin's first 'hypercar', inspired by James Bond

ASTON MARTIN

- The 77 cars were built between 2009 and 2012.
- The car's design team was inspired by hi-tech DTM racing cars.
- Buyers had to pay a deposit of £200,000 when they placed their order.
- The cars have a carbon-fibre monocoque and hand-shaped aluminium body.

**A**ston Martins are already pretty special, and most people think of them as supercars, so how do you go one better? Well, in 2008, Aston Martin decided to build a 'hypercar' as a new flagship for its range, with a 7.2-litre, 750bhp (559kW) V12 engine, and a 220mph top speed. The result was the incredible One-77, which cost £1.2 million when new, and is even more valuable today!

This was Aston Martin's answer to the equally extreme Bugatti Veyron and Ferrari Enzo. The car's name, One-77, was probably chosen as a reference to the most famous Aston Martin driver, James Bond (agent number 007). It also indicated that only 77 cars would be built. In case the One-77 wasn't exclusive enough for some owners, seven were produced as special Q-Series cars, which allowed the wealthy owners to order their cars with special custom paint schemes and interior trim. Q-Series was a reference to the quartermaster at the British Secret Service who provided James Bond's amazing spy gadgets – known as 'Q'.

# STATISTICS ASTON MARTIN ONE-77

| | |
|---|---|
| **Price (new)** | £1.2 million |
| **Max speed** | Over 220mph (354kph) |
| **0–62mph (0–100kph)** | Under 3.7s |
| **Engine type** | Alloy, quad-cam, 48-valve, normally aspirated V12 |
| **Engine capacity** | 7,312cc |
| **Max power** | 750bhp (559kW) |
| **Max torque** | 750Nm (553 lb ft) |
| **Transmission** | Rear-mounted 6-speed automated manual gearbox, carbon-fibre propeller shaft, limited-slip differential |
| **Suspension** | Front and rear double wishbones, front and rear anti-roll bars, pushrod-actuated coil springs and adjustable monotube dampers. Electrically adjustable for ride-height and rate change |
| **Wheels and tyres** | 20in forged alloy front and rear wheels; 255/35 ZR20 front tyres; 335/30 ZR20 rear tyres |
| **Kerb weight** | 1,630kg |
| **Length** | 4,601mm |
| **Width** | 2,204mm including mirrors |
| **Height** | 1,222mm |
| **Year introduced** | 2009 |

AN AUTOMATIC REAR SPOILER IS RAISED AT SPEEDS OVER 100MPH.

# ASTON MARTIN VALKYRIE

A two-seater road car designed by one of the greatest F1 designers

- ➤ 150 road cars and 25 track versions will be built.
- ➤ The Valkyrie AMR Pro track car is designed to lap a track as fast as an F1 car!
- ➤ The car has two huge underbody venturi to create downforce.
- ➤ All the cars were already sold before they were built.

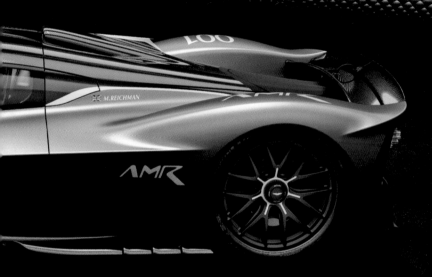

The Valkyrie is a joint project between Aston Martin and Red Bull Technology. One of the big selling points of the car is that Red Bull designer Adrian Newey, who has so far designed ten World Championship-winning F1 cars, has played a big part in the design. The Valkyrie is closer to a road-going F1 car than an extreme sports car.

The Valkyrie's whole structure is carbon-fibre, and to save weight, not a single steel part is used in the car. Active suspension keeps the car flat to the road to improve aerodynamics. An F1-style steering wheel is supplied, with a built-in information display, and most of the car's controls are positioned on the wheel. Instead of mirrors, two rear-facing cameras are used, with displays on each side of the dashboard. The amazing V12 engine is designed to rev to 11,000rpm, and uses technology from a V8 engine that engine-building company Cosworth designed for use in F1 cars. The Valkyrie could be one of the most desirable hypercars ever built!

# STATISTICS ASTON MARTIN VALKYRIE

| | |
|---|---|
| **Price (new)** | £2–3 million |
| **Max speed** | Target 250mph+ (402kph+) |
| **0–60mph (0–97kph)** | Target 2.5s |
| **Engine type** | Naturally aspirated V12 developed by Cosworth |
| **Engine capacity** | 6.5 litres |
| **Max power** | 1,000bhp (746kW) from V12 engine, plus 160bhp (119kW) from KERS electric motor, giving a total of 1,160bhp (865kW) at 10,500rpm |
| **Max torque** | 740Nm (546lb ft) maximum from V12, plus 280Nm (207lb ft) maximum from electric motor, and a combined total of 900Nm (664lb ft) at 6,000rpm |
| **Transmission** | 7-speed paddle-shift gearbox |
| **Suspension** | Wishbones front and rear, with electronically controlled active ride |
| **Wheels and tyres** | 20in front wheels; 21in rear wheels; 265/35 R20 front tyres; 325/30 R21 rear tyres |
| **Kerb weight** | Target 1,000kg |
| **Length** | Unknown |
| **Width** | Unknown |
| **Height** | Unknown |
| **Year introduced** | 2019 |

THE ASTON MARTIN BADGE ON THE NOSE IS THINNER THAN A HUMAN HAIR!

# BAC MONO

A race-inspired single-seater for the ultimate driving experience

- Options include a carbon crash helmet and bespoke Mono race suit pack.
- The sequential gearbox takes 35 milliseconds to complete a gear change.
- The Mono's cockpit controls include a touch-sensitive engine starter button.
- The leather interior trim is specially waterproofed.

I n 2009, brothers Neill and Ian Briggs founded BAC (Briggs Automotive Company), to produce the Mono – a very lightweight, hi-tech, single-seater sports car with stunning performance. The central driving position is designed to make the driver feel part of the car, and the seat and pedal positions are customised for each owner. No in-car entertainment, air conditioning or satnav though...

The car is built using carbon-fibre over a steel safety cell, with a carbon-fibre nose section providing a small storage compartment and front crash protection. The body panels are designed to expose the Mono's mechanical components to reinforce the racing-car styling, and to provide cooling air to the car's engine and radiators. Other features inspired by racing-car technology include the fully adjustable suspension five-point racing harness, detachable steering wheel and adjustable pedals. For owners keen to take their cars on the track, options include a carbon-ceramic brake kit, track-specific gear sets, lightweight exhaust system and carbon wheel rims.

# STATISTICS BAC MONO

| | |
|---|---|
| Price (new) | £167,940 |
| Max speed | 170mph (274kph) |
| 0–60mph (0–97kph) | 2.8s |
| Engine type | Mountune-developed, normally aspirated 4-cylinder, with double-overhead camshafts, variable valve timing |
| Engine capacity | 2,488cc |
| Max power | 305bhp (227kW) at 8,000rpm |
| Max torque | 308Nm (227lb ft) |
| Transmission | 6-speed Formula-3-specification sequential gearbox with limited-slip differential |
| Suspension | Double wishbones front and rear with bellcranks and pushrod-activated spring/damper units, rising rate and adjustable camber |
| Wheels and tyres | 17in front and rear wheels; 205/40 R17 front tyres; 245/40 R17 rear tyres |
| Kerb weight | 580kg |
| Length | 3,952mm |
| Width | 1,836mm |
| Height | 1,110mm |
| Year introduced | 2011 |

THE CAR HAS NO WINDSCREEN, SO A CRASH HELMET IS ESSENTIAL!

# BUGATTI DIVO

A rare and extreme Bugatti built for high-speed cornering

- The car is finished in bare carbon, with grey and 'Divo Racing Blue' paint.
- The Divo has 90kg more downforce than the Chiron.
- Speed is limited to stop the risk of the tyres bursting with the extra downforce!
- All 40 cars were sold in one day to owners who had already bought Chirons.

The Bugatti Divo is based on the Bugatti Chiron that replaced the Veyron. Bugatti decided to build the Divo for the company's 110th anniversary in 2019, and only 40 will be built. The car is aimed at track use, with racing-car handling and aerodynamics, but is still road-legal. The Divo costs nearly twice as much as a Chiron!

The car is slimmer than the Veyron and Chiron. The front air intake is much bigger, for cooling, and a huge front splitter is fitted. The headlights are higher up than other Bugattis, and are ultra-slim to leave more space for brake-cooling ducts. A large air duct in the roof guides air towards the big rear wing. The wing is wider than the Chiron's, and acts as a huge airbrake by tilting forwards when the car is braking. The car is named after Albert Divo, a pilot and mechanic before he won the famous Targa Florio race in Italy twice in the 1920s in a Bugatti Type 35 racing car.

# STATISTICS BUGATTI DIVO

| | |
|---|---|
| **Price (new)** | £4.5 million |
| **Max speed** | Limited to 236mph (380kph) |
| **0–62mph (0–100kph)** | 2.4s |
| **Engine type** | 64-valve, quad-cam W16, quad turbochargers with intercoolers |
| **Engine capacity** | 7,993cc |
| **Max power** | 1,500bhp (1,103kW) at 6,700rpm |
| **Max torque** | 1,600Nm (1,180lb ft) at 2,000–6,000rpm |
| **Transmission** | 7-speed twin-clutch Direct Shift Gearbox (DSG), four-wheel drive, regulated limited-slip differential |
| **Suspension** | Double wishbones front and rear |
| **Wheels and tyres** | 20in front wheels; 21in rear wheels; 285/30 R20 front tyres; 355/25 R21 rear tyres |
| **Kerb weight** | 1,961kg |
| **Length** | 4,641mm |
| **Width** | 2,018mm |
| **Height** | 1,212mm |
| **Year introduced** | 2018 |

THE DIVO'S COOL REAR LIGHTS ARE PARTLY MADE BY 3D PRINTING.

# BUGATTI VEYRON SUPER SPORT

## The Super Sport delivers stunning performance

- The Super Sport's extra power comes from bigger turbochargers.
- The Veyron is named after French Bugatti racing driver Pierre Veyron.
- The Veyron has a total of 10 radiators, including three turbo intercoolers.
- Cristiano Ronaldo, Simon Cowell and Arnold Schwarzenegger own Veyrons.

The Bugatti Veyron first appeared in 2005, and stunned the car world with its amazing 987bhp (736kW) 8.0-litre W12 engine, complete with four turbochargers, and its incredible 253mph (407kph) top speed. But this extreme performance comes at a price. A routine service for a Veyron costs £14,000, and a set of four new tyres costs £23,500!

The Veyron was designed and developed by the Volkswagen-Audi group that owns Bugatti, and was built in Molsheim, France – the historical home of Bugatti cars. In 2010, Bugatti built 30 Veyron Super Sport models with an uprated engine producing 1,184bhp (883kW). In 2013, the Super Sport set a new Guinness World Record as the fastest road-legal production car in the world, reaching 268mph (431kph), though production versions are limited to a maximum of 258mph (415kph). To celebrate the speed record, five Veyron Super Sport World Record Editions were built, with a black carbon body, orange detailing, orange wheels and the electronic speed limiter removed. A luxury hypercar, built for comfort as well as ultimate speed.

# STATISTICS BUGATTI VEYRON SUPER SPORT

| | |
|---|---|
| **Price (new)** | £1.7 million |
| **Max speed** | 268mph (431kph) |
| **0–62mph (0–100kph)** | 2.5s |
| **Engine type** | 64-valve, quad-cam W16, quad turbochargers with intercoolers |
| **Engine capacity** | 7,993cc |
| **Max power** | 1,200bhp (882kW) at 6,400rpm |
| **Max torque** | 1,500Nm (1,106lb ft) at 3,000–5,000rpm |
| **Transmission** | 7-speed twin-clutch Direct Shift Gearbox (DSG), four-wheel drive, regulated limited-slip differential |
| **Suspension** | Double wishbones front and rear |
| **Wheels and tyres** | 520mm front wheels; 540mm rear wheels; 245/690 R520 front tyres; 365/710 R540 rear tyres |
| **Kerb weight** | 1,838kg |
| **Length** | 4,462mm |
| **Width** | 1,998mm |
| **Height** | 1,190mm |
| **Year introduced** | 2010 |

AT FULL SPEED, A VEYRON COULD ONLY RUN FOR 12 MINUTES ON A FULL TANK!

# CAPARO T1

Close as you can get to a road-legal F1 car, with performance to match

- A T1 was painted in police force colours as a futuristic Rapid Response Vehicle!
- A small 'aeroscreen' or a bubble canopy, like a fighter plane, can be fitted.
- A magazine road-tester managed 0–100mph (0–161kph) in 6.2s in a T1.
- Production stopped in 2015, but the car is due to be relaunched as the T1 Evo.

The T1 was originally called the Freestream T1, but the project was bought by the Caparo Vehicle Technologies company and renamed before it went into production in 2007. The car was designed by two engineers who worked on the McLaren F1 road-car project and decided to produce a car that was as close as possible to a road-legal F1 racing car.

The engine is a 3.5-litre V8 that is based on a detuned IndyCar racing engine, and a carbon-fibre and aluminium-honeycomb monocoque chassis is used. The car even has a ground-effect rear diffuser like an F1 car, and the front and rear wings are adjustable to tune the aerodynamics. To complete the racing-car features, a quick-release steering wheel is used, along with racing harnesses for the driver and passenger, and a data-logging system. The car is a two-seater, with side-by-side seats, but the passenger sits slightly further back than the driver so that their shoulders overlap, which means that the car can be narrower.

# STATISTICS CAPARO T1

| | |
|---|---|
| **Price (new)** | £211,000 |
| **Max speed** | 205mph (330kph) |
| **0–62mph (0–100kph)** | 2.5s |
| **Engine type** | Normally aspirated V8 |
| **Engine capacity** | 3,496cc |
| **Max power** | 575bhp (429kW) at 10,500rpm |
| **Max torque** | 420Nm (310lb ft) at 9,000rpm |
| **Transmission** | 6-speed sequential gearbox, limited-slip differential |
| **Suspension** | Double wishbones front and rear with adjustable racing spring/damper units |
| **Wheels and tyres** | 18in front wheels; 19in rear wheels; 235/40 R18 front tyres; 295/30 R19 rear tyres |
| **Kerb weight** | 470kg |
| **Length** | 4,066mm |
| **Width** | 1,990mm |
| **Height** | 1,076mm |
| **Year introduced** | 2007 |

SO FAR, ONLY AROUND 20 T1S HAVE BEEN SOLD AROUND THE WORLD.

# CATERHAM 620R

The original lightweight sports car with supercharged performance

- The standard 620R carbon seats have no padding.
- Standard and large chassis are available to suit drivers of all shapes and sizes.
- The 620R is the fastest production road car Caterham has ever built.
- The 620S model has 620R performance, but comforts such as a clip-on hood!

GN13 GZA

GB

**T**he first Caterham 7 appeared in 1973, and was developed
from the Lotus 7 designed by legendary F1-car designer Colin
Chapman. Over the 45 years since the first Caterham appeared,
the cars have got more and more powerful, faster, and slightly
crazier, and the 620R is a giant-slayer with its performance!

Colin Chapman designed the Lotus 7 in 1957, and since Caterham
began building the car the basic design has hardly changed. All
Caterham models are built for fun, and are like grown-up go-
karts to drive. The cars are available in kit form for buyers to build
themselves, or are fully built by the factory. The chassis is tubular
steel with aluminium-sheet body panels, and glass-fibre nose and
wing panels, but the 620R – aimed at track driving, but road legal –
has a weight-saving carbon-fibre nose and wings, carbon seats and
a carbon dashboard. An immobiliser and removable steering wheel
are fitted as standard, but a heater, adjustable leather seats and a
windscreen are optional extras.

# STATISTICS CATERHAM 620R

| | |
|---|---|
| Price (new) | £48,900 (fully built) |
| Max speed | 155mph (250kph) |
| 0–62mph (0–100kph) | 2.8s |
| Engine type | Supercharged Ford Duratec 4-cylinder |
| Engine capacity | 1,999cc |
| Max power | 310bhp (231kW) at 7,700rpm |
| Max torque | 219Nm (162lb ft) at 7,350rpm |
| Transmission | 6-speed sequential gearbox, limited-slip differential |
| Suspension | Front double wishbones, de Dion rear suspension, adjustable dampers |
| Wheels and tyres | 13in front and rear wheels; 185/55 R13 front tyres; 215/55 R13 rear tyres |
| Kerb weight | 610kg |
| Length | 3,100mm |
| Width | 1,685mm |
| Height | 1,015mm |
| Year introduced | 2013 |

*TOP GEAR MAGAZINE CALLED THE 620R: '... MAD AS A BOX OF FROGS'!*

# FERRARI FXX

A track-only, race-bred car that will never actually be raced!

- The last FXX was presented to Ferrari F1 driver Michael Schumacher.
- The Evoluzione package increased power to 848bhp (632kW) at 9,500rpm.
- All owners were presented with a 'free' helmet to match their car's colours.
- Data from the FXX programme was used to develop the Ferrari LaFerrari.

The Ferrari FXX was developed from the 2002 Enzo, named after Ferrari's founder Enzo Ferrari. At the time, the Enzo was the quickest-ever road-going Ferrari, with a 6.0-litre V12 engine, F1-style gearbox, carbon-fibre body, traction control and F1-influenced aerodynamics. Ferrari decided to make the Enzo go even faster for a lucky 38 customers, but only for track use.

The FXX was designed for the track, but not for racing. Ferrari offered the cars to a few selected existing customers, and part of the buying agreement was that Ferrari engineers must check the car before it can be driven anywhere! The car is called FXX because it is part of Ferrari's 'XX' programme, which enables the cars' owners to 'arrive and drive' their cars at special track days organised by Ferrari. Ferrari engineers and professional test drivers are at these sessions to run the cars and coach the owners. In 2009, Ferrari introduced an 'Evoluzione' package for the FXX, making it even quicker thanks to aerodynamic chang,es and engine and gearbox improvements.

# STATISTICS FERRARI FXX

| | |
|---|---|
| Price (new) | £2 million |
| Max speed | 214mph (345kph) |
| 0–60mph (0–97kph) | Unknown |
| Engine type | Normally aspirated 48-valve V12 |
| Engine capacity | 6,262cc |
| Max power | 800bhp (588kW) at 8,500rpm |
| Max torque | 686Nm (506lb ft) at 5,750rpm |
| Transmission | Electro-hydraulic F1-style 6-speed gearbox |
| Suspension | Double wishbones front and rear with pushrod-operated spring/damper units |
| Wheels and tyres | 19in front and rear wheels; 245/35 R19 front tyres; 345/35 R19 rear tyres |
| Kerb weight | 1,155kg |
| Length | 4,832mm |
| Width | 2,040mm |
| Height | 1,127mm |
| Year introduced | 2005 |

ONE UK FXX OWNER HAD HIS CAR CONVERTED BY FERRARI TO BE ROAD-LEGAL.

# FERRARI FXX-K EVO

**Ferrari's hybrid-powered 'XX' car; technology for the future**

- All 'XX' cars are kept by Ferrari – owners can't take them home.
- An active rear spoiler is fitted, which lifts to slow the car under braking.
- The EVO produces 830kg of downforce at the car's top speed.
- Engineers collect data from the cars' track sessions for use in future Ferraris.

The FXX-K, built between 2015 and 2017, is based on the car that was designed to be the ultimate Ferrari – the LaFerrari that translates to *The* Ferrari in English. Obviously, Ferrari decided that it wasn't 'ultimate' enough! The FXX-K was Ferrari's first hybrid car, powered by a 6,262cc V12 engine coupled to a HY-KERS hybrid system, giving a total power of 950bhp (708kW).

The FXX-K is a track-only car, which is part of Ferrari's 'XX' track-day programme. Ferrari produced 40 FXX-Ks, each car costing an estimated £2 million! In late 2017, Ferrari announced a special upgrade 'EVO' aerodynamic package for the FXX-K, which increases the car's downforce by a huge 23 per cent (while also reducing the weight of the car), using revised bodywork and a full-size rear wing. The EVO also has special tyre-monitoring sensors that record how the tyres interact with the track, as well as their temperatures and pressures. The FXX-K EVO is quicker on the track than many racing cars, and sounds incredible!

# STATISTICS FERRARI FXX-K EVO

| | |
|---|---|
| Price (new) | No official price, but more than £2.4 million |
| Max speed | 217mph (349kph) |
| 0–60mph (0–97kph) | Unknown |
| Engine type | Normally aspirated V12 internal combustion engine, plus HY-KERS electric motor |
| Engine capacity | 6,262cc |
| Max power | 860bhp (641kW) at 9,200rpm for V12 engine, plus 187bhp (140kW) from HY-KERS system, giving a total of 1,047bhp (781kW) |
| Max torque | 750Nm (553lb ft) at 6,500rpm from internal combustion engine, total torque including HY-KERS over 900Nm (664lb ft) |
| Transmission | 7-speed dual-clutch gearbox, with electronic differential |
| Suspension | Front double wishbones, rear multi-link, with 'magnetorheological' damping |
| Wheels and tyres | 19in front wheels; 20in rear wheels; 285/650 R19 front tyres; 345/725 R20 rear tyres |
| Kerb weight | 1,405kg |
| Length | 4,896mm |
| Width | 2,051mm |
| Height | 1,116mm |
| Year introduced | 2015 |

THIS CAR IS EVEN MORE POWERFUL THAN FERRARI'S CURRENT F1 CAR.

# KOENIGSEGG AGERA RS

A record-breaking hi-tech hypercar from Sweden

- The car's wheels are made from carbon-fibre.
- One car was built with 24-carat gold-leaf bodywork and engine bay trim!
- An optional '1-Megawatt' package increases power to 1,241bhp (1,000kW).
- Three customers have given their cars names: 'Draken', 'Gryphon' and 'Phoenix'.

The Agera RS is aimed at track driving, but still has features that make it suitable for use on the road, such as air conditioning, satnav and a removable roof panel. The car has special lightweight parts and high-downforce aerodynamics, and in 2017 it set a new world speed record for a production car of 277.9mph (447.2kph)!

The original Koenigsegg Agera appeared in 2011, with a 5.0-litre V8 twin-turbo engine and a top speed of 249mph (400kph). The car has a carbon-fibre chassis and carbon bodywork. Agera R and Agera S models followed, with more power and an electronically controlled active rear wing. The extra-lightweight Agera RS appeared in 2015, combining the equipment from the 'R' and 'S' models with extra features, including side skirts and an underbody flap system to improve aerodynamics, plus a built-in hydraulic jacking system so that it can be driven over speed bumps and kerbs. All 25 Agera RS models were hand-built to each individual customer's specifications, making each one unique.

# STATISTICS KOENIGSEGG AGERA RS

| | |
|---|---|
| **Price (new)** | £2 million |
| **Max speed** | 284mph (457kph) |
| **0–60mph (0–97kph)** | 2.9s |
| **Engine type** | Twin-turbo V8 |
| **Engine capacity** | 5.0 litres |
| **Max power** | 1,160bhp (865kW) at 7,800rpm |
| **Max torque** | 1,280Nm (944lb ft) at 4,100rpm |
| **Transmission** | 7-speed paddle-shift gearbox, Koenigsegg electronic differential |
| **Suspension** | Wishbones with electronically adjustable dampers front and rear, and additional pushrod-operated 'Triplex' damper at rear |
| **Wheels and tyres** | 19in front wheels; 20in rear wheels; 265/35 R19 front tyres; 345/30 R20 rear tyres |
| **Kerb weight** | 1,395kg |
| **Length** | 4,293mm |
| **Width** | 2,050mm |
| **Height** | 1,120mm |
| **Year introduced** | 2015 |

ONE OWNER SOLD HIS CAR AFTER FIVE MONTHS FOR A PROFIT OF NEARLY £1.5 MILLION!

# KOENIGSEGG JESKO

## The best so far from a company that has builds only hypercars

➤ Jeskos are available in high-downforce (track) and low-drag (road) versions.

➤ A G-force meter can be fitted on the dashboard as an option.

➤ The 'Smartwheel' steering wheel has two small touchscreens built in.

➤ Koenigsegg's factory codename for the car was 'Ragnorok'!

The Jesko has a specially designed twin-turbo 5.0-litre 1,600bhp (1,193kW) V8 engine and hi-tech computer systems, and is designed to excel on the track. Although it has high-downforce aerodynamics and race-inspired suspension, it will be road-legal, with plenty of creature comforts for the driver!

Specialist Swedish hypercar builder Koenigsegg unveiled the stunning Jesko at the Geneva Motor Show in March 2019. The car has been developed from the Koenigsegg Agera, and is named after the father of company, founder Christian von Koenigsegg. Advanced electronic systems include a 'SmartCenter' instrument display (which has a copy of the car's owners' manual installed) that rotates with the steering wheel. The display's centre section turns to keep the vital gauges level for easy reading. A 'UPOD' (Ultimate Power On Demand) system automatically selects the best gear for maximum acceleration. The system can jump gears without needing to change gear in sequence. The first production cars will be available in 2020, but all 125 are already sold.

# STATISTICS KOENIGSEGG JESKO

| | |
|---|---|
| **Price (new)** | Around £2.5 million |
| **Max speed** | Target 300mph (483kph) |
| **0–60mph (0–97kph)** | Unknown |
| **Engine type** | Twin-turbo V8 |
| **Engine capacity** | 5.0 litres |
| **Max power** | 1,600bhp (1,193kW) on E85 biofuel; 1,280bhp (209kW) on standard fuel |
| **Max torque** | 1,500Nm (1,106lb ft) at 5,100rpm |
| **Transmission** | 9-speed Koenigsegg Light Speed Transmission (LST) |
| **Suspension** | Wishbones with electronically controlled 'Triplex' three-damper system front and rear |
| **Wheels and tyres** | 20in front wheels; 21in rear wheels; 265/35 R20 front tyres; 345/30 R21 rear tyres |
| **Kerb weight** | 1,420kg |
| **Length** | 4,610mm |
| **Width** | 2,030mm |
| **Height** | 1,210mm |
| **Year introduced** | 2020 |

THE FACTORY IN SWEDEN CAN ADJUST THE SUSPENSION DAMPERS ONLINE!

# KTM X-BOW RR

A two-seater that looks like it belongs in a Transformers movie

- The X-Bow has been used in the all-star Race of Champions event since 2008.
- The quick-release steering wheel can be removed to get in and out of the car.
- Like an F1 car, a separate front carbon/aluminium crash structure is fitted.
- KTM recommends that a helmet is worn when driving the X-Bow.

The X-Bow (pronounced 'crossbow') is built for a raw driving experience! It has a carbon-composite chassis based on a Formula 3 racing-car monocoque. There is no windscreen, or doors, but it does have two seats and a turbocharged Audi 2.0-litre 360bhp (268kW) engine. An optional luggage bag straps on to the bodywork behind the seats.

The X-Bow is the first, and so far only, car produced by Austrian motorcycle manufacturer KTM. The car has been available since 2008, and various models have been built, with the most extreme model – the RR ('Race Ready') – appearing in 2012. The RR has a more powerful engine than other models in the range, and the engine/gearbox is lowered for better weight distribution. Buyers can choose from a range of options to customise their car and its performance, including special motorsport parts. For drivers who want even more thrills, several 'one-make' racing series are run especially for the X-Bow.

# STATISTICS KTM X-BOW RR

| | |
|---|---|
| Price (new) | Starts at around £87,000 |
| Max speed | Approximately 145mph (233kph) |
| 0–62mph (0–100kph) | 3.3s |
| Engine type | Audi TFSI 4-cylinder DOHC, direct injection, turbocharged with intercooler |
| Engine capacity | 1,984cc |
| Max power | 360bhp (268kW) at 6,400rpm |
| Max torque | 420Nm (310lb ft) at 3,200rpm |
| Transmission | 6-speed manual gearbox, limited slip differential |
| Suspension | Double wishbones front and rear with pushrod-operated coil spring/damper units |
| Wheels and tyres | 17in front wheels; 18in rear wheels; 215/45 R17 front tyres; 255/35 R18 rear tyres |
| Kerb weight | 810kg |
| Length | 3,738mm |
| Width | 1,915mm |
| Height | 1,202mm |
| Year introduced | 2012 |

MOST OF THE CAR'S SWITCHES ARE MOUNTED ON THE STEERING WHEEL.

# LAMBORGHINI VENENO

The most exclusive and expensive Lamborghini so far

- The Veneno is named after a famous and powerful fighting bull.
- Lamborghini kept a Veneno coupé as a birthday present to itself.
- Lamborghini developed 'Rosso Veneno' paint especially for the roadster.
- At £3.3 million, the Veneno roadster costs the same as three Bugatti Veyrons!

The stunning Veneno is based on the Lamborghini Aventador, but has a more powerful engine and redesigned bodywork inspired by the styling of LMP1 sports racing cars. Only three coupé and nine roadster versions have been built, taking the final number of production Venenos build to 11 – pretty exclusive!

Lamborghini announced the Veneno in 2013 to celebrate the 50th anniversary of the company. The original Veneno was a coupé, and after two prototypes were built, only three production cars were made, and all were sold before they were finished. The bodywork is designed to optimise the car's aerodynamics. The whole front of the car acts as a huge wing, and the flat underbody has a large downforce-producing rear diffuser, like those found on racing cars. Lamborghini announced the roadster version of the Veneno in 2014, unveiling the car spectacularly on an Italian Navy aircraft carrier docked in Abu Dhabi. The Veneno roadster became the most expensive production car ever built, at £3.3 million!

# STATISTICS LAMBORGHINI VENENO

| | |
|---|---|
| **Price (new)** | £3 million (coupé) or £3.3 million (roadster) |
| **Max speed** | 221mph (355kph) |
| **0–62mph (0–100kph)** | 2.8s |
| **Engine type** | Normally aspirated V12 |
| **Engine capacity** | 6,498cc |
| **Max power** | 750bhp (552kW) at 8,400rpm |
| **Max torque** | 690Nm (509lb ft) at 5,500rpm |
| **Transmission** | 7-speed semi-automatic gearbox, four-wheel-drive, mechanical limited-slip differential |
| **Suspension** | Double wishbones from and rear, with pushrod-operated spring/damper units |
| **Wheels and tyres** | 20in front wheels; 21in rear wheels; 255/30 R20 front tyres; 355/25 R21 rear tyres |
| **Kerb weight** | 1,450kg |
| **Length** | 5,020mm |
| **Width** | 2,075mm |
| **Height** | 1,165mm |
| **Year introduced** | 2013 |

IN 2016, A USED VENENO COUPÉ WAS UP FOR SALE FOR 8.8 MILLION POUNDS!

# LOTUS 3-ELEVEN 430

**A big engine in a small car for maximum excitement**

- Just 20 3-Eleven 430s will be built out of a total of 311 3-Eleven models.
- The 3-Eleven 430 is the fastest road-going car ever to lap Lotus's test track.
- The car is supplied with semi-slick tyres as standard.
- Built for the track, the car has just enough equipment to make it road legal.

The Lotus 3-Eleven is the most extreme and expensive Lotus road car yet built. In early 2018, Lotus announced that the final 20 cars to be built would be upgraded '430' models. These cars are powered by a supercharged 3.5-litre, 430bhp (321kW) Toyota V6 – a hugely powerful engine for a car as small as the 3-Eleven.

The 3-Eleven has a bonded aluminium chassis, with built-in rollover protection, and lightweight carbon-composite bodywork and interior panels. The '430' has a rear wing mounted higher up than that of the standard 3-Eleven, and a modified front splitter that increases the car's aerodynamic downforce to improve grip. Reviewers say that the 3-Eleven is one of the best-handling and most exciting sports cars ever built. The car has very basic controls – a digital display, a steering-column stalk for the indicators and headlight main beam, a small carbon-fibre control panel that contains the starter button, fire extinguisher button, battery isolation switch, headlight, fog light and hazard flasher switches, and that's all!

# STATISTICS LOTUS 3-ELEVEN 430

| | |
|---|---|
| **Price (new)** | £102,000 |
| **Max speed** | 180mph (290kph) |
| **0–62mph (0–100kph)** | 3.2s |
| **Engine type** | Toyota 24-valve V6, supercharged with intercooler |
| **Engine capacity** | 3,456cc |
| **Max power** | 430bhp (321kW) at 7,000rpm |
| **Max torque** | 440Nm (325lb ft) at 4,500rpm |
| **Transmission** | 6-speed manual gearbox, limited-slip differential, variable traction control |
| **Suspension** | Double wishbones front and rear with adjustable dampers |
| **Wheels and tyres** | 18in front wheels; 19in rear wheels; 225/40 R18 front tyres; 275/30 R19 rear tyres |
| **Kerb weight** | 920kg |
| **Length** | 4,120mm |
| **Width** | 1,860mm |
| **Height** | 1,200mm |
| **Year introduced** | 2018 |

THE '430' ADDITION TO THE NAME INDICATES ITS 430BHP (321KW) POWER.

# McLAREN F1

The original 'hypercar', still a sensation more than 25 years on

- The F1 is a three-seater with a central driver's seat.
- To cope with the heat from the engine, the engine bay is lined with pure gold!
- The on-board toolkit is made from titanium – half the weight of steel.
- The F1 is still the fastest normally-aspirated road car ever built.

The McLaren F1 may be over 25 years old, but it is the original 'hypercar', and still one of the most sought-after cars in the world. Ferraris, Lamborghinis and Porsches had ruled the supercar world until the F1 appeared, but the McLaren set new standards that would not be beaten for years.

At the time the F1 was built, the McLaren team dominated Formula 1 racing, and the company decided to build the world's ultimate road car. Almost no expense was spared. The F1 was the first road car with a carbon-fibre chassis, each of which took more than 3,000 hours to make. Amazingly, a racing version of the F1 – the F1 GTR – won the Le Mans 24-Hour race in 1995 at its first attempt, taking four of the top five places! To mark the win, McLaren built five F1 LM road-going versions and, later, three F1 GTs based on the F1 GTR 'Longtail' racing car. Many people think that the F1 is the greatest road car ever built!

# STATISTICS MCLAREN F1

| | |
|---|---|
| Price (new) | £540,000 |
| Max speed | 240.1mph (386.4kph) |
| 0–62mph (0–100kph) | 3.2s |
| Engine type | BMW normally aspirated V12 |
| Engine capacity | 6,064cc |
| Max power | 618bhp (461kW) |
| Max torque | 650Nm (479lb ft) |
| Transmission | 6-speed manual gearbox, limited-slip differential |
| Suspension | Double wishbones front and rear with Bilstein spring/gas damper units |
| Wheels and tyres | 17in front and rear wheels; 235/45 R17 front tyres; 315/45 R17 rear tyres |
| Kerb weight | 1,138kg |
| Length | 4,287mm |
| Width | 1,820mm |
| Height | 1,140mm |
| Year introduced | 1992 |

INCLUDING PROTOTYPES AND RACING CARS, ONLY 106 CARS WERE EVER BUILT.

# McLAREN P1

## Stunning looks and a superhero performance to match

- 375 standard P1s were built, along with just over 40 GTRs and five LMs.
- F1 Champion Jenson Button sold his P1 with only 551 miles on the clock.
- The P1 can be driven for 12 miles at 30mph using just the electric motor
- The P1 comes with air conditioning, satnav and audio system, but mats are an extra!

The McLaren P1 followed in the footsteps of the incredible McLaren F1, and its stunning styling maximises aerodynamic performance. Describing the car's shape, its designer, Frank Stephenson said: 'It's as though we stuck a tube inside and sucked all the air out…' This extreme car was tested in extreme conditions, in the cold of the Arctic Circle and the heat of Death Valley!

The car has a Drag Reduction System (DRS), as used on F1 cars, that reduces the car's aerodynamic drag when a button on the steering wheel is pressed to move the rear wing flat. The Instant Power Assist System (IPAS) is an electric motor that works automatically to boost engine power, or can be operated by a button on the steering wheel. In 2015, McLaren introduced the P1 GTR – a track-only version with power increased to 986bhp (735kW), and built-in air jacks! The ultra-rare road-legal P1 LM uses the same 986bhp engine as the GTR, but has special lightweight components, improved aerodynamics, and no air jacks.

# STATISTICS MCLAREN P1

| | |
|---|---|
| **Price (new)** | £866,000 |
| **Max speed** | 217mph (350kph) |
| **0–62mph (0–100kph)** | 2.8s |
| **Engine type** | Twin-turbo V8 internal combustion engine, plus IPAS electric motor |
| **Engine capacity** | 3,799cc |
| **Max power** | 727bhp (542kW) for V8 engine, plus 176bhp (131kW) from IPAS electric motor, giving a total of 903bhp (673kW) |
| **Max torque** | 720Nm (531lb ft) from internal combustion engine, plus 260Nm (192lb ft) from IPAS electric motor, giving a total of 980Nm (723lb ft) |
| **Transmission** | 7-speed dual-clutch gearbox |
| **Suspension** | Double wishbones front and rear with Race Active Chassis Control (RCC) |
| **Wheels and tyres** | 19in front wheels; 20in rear wheels; 245/35 R19 front tyres; 315/30 R20 rear tyres |
| **Kerb weight** | 1,547kg |
| **Length** | 4,588mm |
| **Width** | 1,946mm |
| **Height** | 1,188mm |
| **Year introduced** | 2013 |

THE P1 GTR WAS OFFERED ONLY TO OWNERS WHO HAD ALREADY BOUGHT A P1.

# McLAREN SENNA

## A worthy tribute to a legendary F1 driver

- Named after three-time World Champion McLaren F1 driver Ayrton Senna.
- The monocoque chassis and bodywork are made from carbon-fibre.
- Special black paint is used to reduce the amount of liquid used, saving weight!
- The active aerodynamics produce 800kg of downforce at 155mph (249kph).

The McLaren Senna is a sensational track-focused car. It is technically road-legal, but it is not aimed at road use – the only luggage space is a small stowage area for two race suits and helmets. No space for shopping or sports kit… It does, however, have a power-operated drink system to keep the driver hydrated!

McLaren's engineers designed this awesome machine to deliver the most intense driving experience of any McLaren road car. They did this by saving weight in every possible area of the car – including hollow carbon-fibre seats and even special lightweight paint! The RaceActive Chassis Control system has a Race mode that lowers the car's ride-height, increasing aerodynamic downforce and stiffening the suspension as the speed increases to cope with the high downforce loads. The system also controls the front and rear spoilers to stabilise the car and provide maximum grip. The car has a data-logging system to record each track lap, and optional extras include six-point racing harnesses for the driver and passenger.

# STATISTICS MCLAREN SENNA

| | |
|---|---|
| Price (new) | £750,000 |
| Max speed | 208mph (335kph) |
| 0–62mph (0–100kph) | 2.8s |
| Engine type | Twin-turbo, alloy 32-valve V8 with twin electrically actuated twin-scroll turbochargers, double-overhead camshafts, variable valve timing |
| Engine capacity | 3,994cc |
| Max power | 789bhp (588kW) at 7,250rpm |
| Max torque | 800Nm (590lb ft) at 5,500–6,700rpm |
| Transmission | 7-speed Seamless Shift Gearbox (SSG) with open differential and Brake Steer |
| Suspension | Double wishbones front and rear with active dampers and RaceActive Chassis Control II system |
| Wheels and tyres | 19in front wheels; 20in rear wheels; 245/35 R19 front tyres; 315/30 R20 rear tyres |
| Kerb weight | 1,309kg |
| Length | 4,744mm |
| Width | 2,153mm |
| Height | 1,195mm |
| Year introduced | 2018 |

THE FOUR CARBON BRAKE DISCS TAKE SEVEN MONTHS EACH TO MANUFACTURE.

# NOBLE M600

A rare hand-built hypercar with giant-slaying performance

- The M600's performance matches that of the McLaren F1 from 0–200mph (322kph).
- The car is available with a manual gearbox or a paddle-shift clutchless option.
- The traction-control button has a protective cover from a Tornado fighter jet.
- M600 owners include F1 World Champion Damon Hill and actor Tom Cruise.

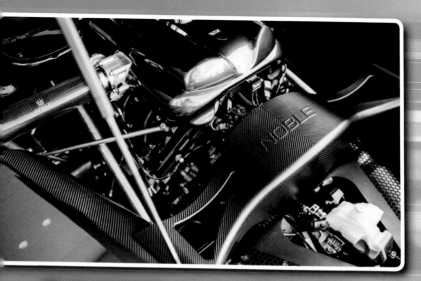

E ach car is bespoke, and is hand-built to the individual customer's requirements. An adjustable turbo-boost switch is fitted, with three settings – 'road', 'track' and 'race', providing 450bhp (336kW), 550bhp (410kW) and 662bhp (494kW). Reviewers have described the M600 as one of the most usable, practical and rewarding hypercars ever built.

Noble Automotive is a British manufacturer that first began producing the M600 in 2010. The car is available in three versions – the Coupé, CarbonSport and Speedster. All the cars have similar mechanical components and performance, but the Coupé is the original car, with painted carbon body panels. The CarbonSport is basically the same Coupé model with a unique coloured carbon finish, with the carbon weave visible – the colour is produced using a special 'ink' added to the finishing lacquer coat. The Speedster has a removable roof panel. A steel and aluminium spaceframe chassis is used, with carbon-fibre body parts.

# STATISTICS NOBLE M600

| | |
|---|---|
| Price (new) | From around £206,000 |
| Max speed | Estimated 225mph (362kph) |
| 0–60mph (0–97kph) | 2.9s |
| Engine type | Yamaha Judd 32-valve, twin-turbo V8 with adjustable boost |
| Engine capacity | 4,439cc |
| Max power | 662bhp (492kW) at 6,500rpm |
| Max torque | 819Nm (604lb ft) at 6,800rpm |
| Transmission | 6-speed manual gearbox, traction control |
| Suspension | Double wishbones front and rear with coil springs over dampers and front and rear anti-roll bars |
| Wheels and tyres | 19in front wheels; 20in rear wheels; 255/30 R19 front tyres; 335/30 R20 rear tyres |
| Kerb weight | 1,198kg |
| Length | 4,360mm |
| Width | 1,910mm |
| Height | 1,140mm |
| Year introduced | 2010 |

THE M600'S V8 ENGINE IS BASED ON THE UNIT USED IN THE VOLVO XC90.

# PAGANI HUAYRA BC

Specially developed materials for one of the lightest-ever hypercars

- The Huayra is named after Huarya-tata, an Andean wind god.
- One customer ordered a Huarya BC with a factory-fitted cup-holder!
- Racing-car manufacturer Dallara helped to optimise the car's aerodynamics.
- When it first appeared, the Huarya BC was the lightest hypercar available.

**H**oracio Pagani has been a world leader in hypercar design since his first production car – the stunning Zonda C12 – appeared in 1999. The original Huayra coupé appeared in 2011. The Huayra BC has the same roof panel as the coupé, but almost every other component has been redesigned to save weight. Anything that could be made lighter has been!

The 'BC' in the car's name stands for Benny Caiola, who was the very first customer to buy a Pagani car. The car was designed to be road-legal, but also super-quick for track days. Each car comes with two sets of wheels and tyres – one for the road and one for the track. The car uses specially developed lightweight materials, including a 'Carbo-Titanium' chassis and 'CrMoVanadio' metal for the front and rear suspension frames. The car's hi-tech systems include active aerodynamics, with flaps that move automatically to stabilise the car and maximise downforce for cornering, and carbon-ceramic brakes. Only 20 Huarya BCs have been built.

# STATISTICS PAGANI HUAYRA BC

| | |
|---|---|
| **Price (new)** | £2 million |
| **Max speed** | Estimated 230mph (370kph) |
| **0–62mph (0–100kph)** | Estimated 2.8s |
| **Engine type** | Mercedes-Benz AMG, twin-turbo V12 |
| **Engine capacity** | 5,980cc |
| **Max power** | 740bhp (552kW) at 6,200rpm |
| **Max torque** | 1,000Nm (738lb ft) at 4,000rpm |
| **Transmission** | 7-speed automated manual transmission with electronic mechanical differential |
| **Suspension** | Double wishbones front and rear with front and rear anti-roll bars, coil springs and adjustable dampers |
| **Wheels and tyres** | 20in front wheels; 21in rear wheels; 255/30 R20 front tyres; 355/25 R21 rear tyres |
| **Kerb weight** | 1,218kg |
| **Length** | 4,605mm |
| **Width** | 2,036mm |
| **Height** | 1,169mm |
| **Year introduced** | 2016 |

THE CAR HAS AN ELECTRIC PARKING BRAKE TO SAVE WEIGHT.

# PAGANI HUAYRA ROADSTER

### The Pagani Huayra Roadster, one of the fastest roofless cars ever

- Electronic active suspension and aerodynamics keep the car stable.
- The lines visible in the carbon-fibre body panels meet in the centre of the car.
- Special Pirelli P Zero Corsa tyres were designed specially for the Roadster.
- The car has a removable roof panel, but there is nowhere in the car to store it!

**W**e have already looked at the Huayra BC, and the Roadster uses some of the BC's hi-tech systems and materials but is a very different car. Even by hypercar standards, the lightweight parts for the Huayra Roadster are extreme, and special 'Carbo-Triax' composite material is used for the bodywork. The result is a weight saving of 80kg compared to the coupé!

Originally, the design of the Huayra Roadster was to be based on the coupé, with a removable roof. However, in 2013, Pagani scrapped this idea and began a completely new design for the Roadster, although the general shape is still similar to that of the coupé. The aim was to make the Roadster lighter – usually, roadster versions of a car are heavier than coupés because they need strengthening due to the lack of roof. The lightweight parts include titanium bolts used throughout the car, each one with a Pagani logo, costing £65 each! The Roadster also has a more powerful engine, making it the most powerful Pagani yet built!

# STATISTICS PAGANI HUAYRA ROADSTER

| | |
|---|---|
| Price (new) | £2.4 million |
| Max speed | 238mph (383kph) |
| 0–60mph (0–97kph) | 2.8s |
| Engine type | Mercedes-Benz AMG, twin-turbo V12 |
| Engine capacity | 5,980cc |
| Max power | 764bhp (562kW) at 5,500rpm |
| Max torque | 1,000Nm (738lb ft) at 2,300–4,300rpm |
| Transmission | 7-speed automated manual transmission with electronic mechanical differential |
| Suspension | Double wishbones front and rear with front and rear anti-roll bars, coil springs and adjustable dampers |
| Wheels and tyres | 20in front wheels; 21in rear wheels; 255/35 ZR20 front tyres; 325/30 ZR21 rear tyres |
| Kerb weight | 1,280kg |
| Length | 4,605mm |
| Width | 2,036mm |
| Height | 1,169mm |
| Year introduced | 2017 |

100 HUAYRA ROADSTERS WILL BE BUILT, ALL TAILOR-MADE FOR THEIR OWNERS.

# PORSCHE CARRERA GT

A hypercar with an F1 engine, and a chassis from a Le Mans winner

- Porsche was originally going to build 1,500 cars, but stopped after 1,270.
- An electronically-operated rear wing lifts at 70mph and closes below 50mph.
- The removable roof panels can be stored in the front luggage compartment.
- A five-piece luggage set was included free, but air conditioning was an extra.

The Porsche Carrera GT first appeared at the Geneva Motor Show in 2000, and went on sale in 2003, but it is still one of the most impressive hypercars ever built. The V10 engine makes an incredible sound – just like an F1 car – and is just as powerful, too.

The Carrera GT's engine is based on an engine that Porsche originally designed for an F1 car, but the engine was never used in F1, and was modified for use in a Le Mans car. The Le Mans car was then cancelled, so it was third time lucky for the engine when Porsche decided to use it in the Carrera GT road car. The Carbon-Fibre Reinforced Plastic (CFRP) chassis was adapted from the chassis used on Porsche's 1998 Le Mans-winning GT1 car. Other racing-car features include a carbon clutch, carbon brakes, and wheels made from magnesium. Colour-coded wheel nuts are fitted – red on the driver's side and blue on the passenger side – because they tighten in opposite directions.

# STATISTICS PORSCHE CARRERA GT

| | |
|---|---|
| Price (new) | £330,000 |
| Max speed | 205mph (330kph) |
| 0–60mph (0–97kph) | 3.5s |
| Engine type | Normally aspirated V10 |
| Engine capacity | 5,733cc |
| Max power | 603bhp (450kW) at 3,000rpm |
| Max torque | 590Nm (435lb ft) at 5,750rpm |
| Transmission | 6-speed manual gearbox |
| Suspension | Double wishbones front and rear, pushrod-operated spring/damper units |
| Wheels and tyres | 19in front wheels; 20in rear wheels; 265/35 R19 front tyres; 335/30 R20 rear tyres |
| Kerb weight | 1,380kg |
| Length | 4,613mm |
| Width | 1,921mm |
| Height | 1,166mm |
| Year introduced | 2003 |

EACH CAR HAS A NUMBERED IDENTIFICATION PLAQUE ON THE CONSOLE.

# PORSCHE 911 GT2 RS

The fastest-ever road-going version of a classic sports car

- A built-in titanium roll-cage protects the driver and passenger.
- Cars are available without a sound system and climate-control to save weight.
- Ceramic brake discs are fitted to reduce weight and improve performance.
- An optional lift system raises the car's front for speed bumps and kerbs.

The Porsche 911 first appeared in 1963, and was an instant classic. The 911 GT2 RS was launched in 2017, over 50 years after the first car appeared, and is the quickest and most powerful 911 yet built. Porsche 911s have become more refined over the years, but this version is raw, noisy and fast!

The huge air intakes at the front of the car cool the engine and brakes, and vents in the bonnet and front and rear wheel arches let the hot air out, also helping to improve the aerodynamics. The car has a lot of weight-saving features, and many of the body parts are made from Carbon-Fibre Reinforced Plastic (CFRP). The roof panel is magnesium, lightweight glass is used, and the twin exhausts are titanium. The catalytic converters glow red at high speeds and when accelerating hard, and can be seen through open holes at the back of the car. Owners can buy a special Porsche Design Chronograph 911 GT2 RS watch, only available to drivers of the 911 GT2 RS!

# STATISTICS PORSCHE 911 GT2 RS

| | |
|---|---|
| Price (new) | £207,506 |
| Max speed | 211mph (340kph) |
| 0–62mph (0–100kph) | 2.8s |
| Engine type | Twin-turbocharged flat-6 |
| Engine capacity | 3,800cc |
| Max power | 691bhp (515kW) at 7,000rpm |
| Max torque | 750Nm (553lb ft) at 2,500–4,500rpm |
| Transmission | 7-speed double-clutch PDK gearbox, rear-wheel drive |
| Suspension | McPherson strut front suspension; multi-link rear suspension |
| Wheels and tyres | 20in front wheels; 21in rear wheels; 265/35 R20 front tyres; 325/30 R21 rear tyres |
| Kerb weight | 1,470kg |
| Length | 4,549mm |
| Width | 1,880mm |
| Height | 1,297mm |
| Year introduced | 2017 |

THE CAR IS TOO NOISY TO TAKE PART IN MOST TRACK DAYS IN THE UK!

# PORSCHE 918 SPYDER

The world's fastest-accelerating production car

- A 'Weissach' package uses lightweight parts to save 41kg, and costs £60,000 extra!
- The 918 Spyder is available in left-hand drive only.
- An optional 'fast charger' charges the hybrid-system battery in 25 minutes.
- In a road test, *Car and Driver* magazine clocked 0–60mph (0–97kph) in 2.2 seconds.

The Porsche 918 Spyder is the fastest Porsche production car yet built. It's a stunning hybrid hypercar powered by a 600bhp (447kW) V8, along with two electric motors. One electric motor drives the front wheels, and the other is coupled with the V8 engine to drive the rear wheels. Optional metallic paint costs an extra £51,400!

The 918 Spyder first appeared as a concept in 2010, and after more than 2,000 possible customers showed interest, Porsche decided to put the car into production. 918 cars were built, and the last one rolled off the production line in June 2015. A one-off 918 RSR 'racing laboratory' was also built, with a coupé body. The RSR was aimed at racing, but is not actually eligible for any racing series! The RSR still has two electric motors, but each motor drives one of the front wheels, while the V8 engine drives the rear wheels. The electric motors don't run all the time, but can provide a 200bhp (150kW) power boost for around 8 seconds.

# STATISTICS PORSCHE 918 SPYDER

| | |
|---|---|
| Price (new) | £781,000 |
| Max speed | 218mph (351kph) |
| 0–62mph (0–100kph) | 2.4s |
| Engine type | Normally aspirated V8, plus two electric motors |
| Engine capacity | 4,593cc |
| Max power | 608bhp (447kW) maximum from V8 engine, plus 286bhp (210kW) maximum from electric motors, and a combined maximum available total of 887bhp (652kW) at 8,500rpm |
| Max torque | 1,280Nm (944lb ft) |
| Transmission | 7-speed PDK gearbox, four-wheel-drive |
| Suspension | Wishbones and links, with Porsche Active Suspension Management (PASM) adaptive dampers |
| Wheels and tyres | 20in front wheels; 21in rear wheels; 265/35 R20 front tyres; 325/30 R21 rear tyres |
| Kerb weight | 1,634kg |
| Length | 4,643mm |
| Width | 1,940mm |
| Height | 1,167mm |
| Year introduced | 2013 |

THE CAR'S DETACHABLE ROOF PANEL CAN BE STORED UNDER THE BONNET.

# SALEEN S7 TWIN TURBO

A thundering V8 supercar built as a racing car, modified for the road

- At 160mph (257kph) the aerodynamics produce the car's own weight in downforce.
- S7s have appeared in Hollywood films *Iron Man*, *Bruce Almighty* and *Redline*.
- Including all racing cars and road models, fewer than 100 S7s have been built.
- The road car has air conditioning, a sound system and a reversing camera.

**A**merican professional racing driver and businessman Steve Saleen developed the original Saleen S7 for racing back in 2000, and because the racing regulations said the car had to be a production car, a few road cars had to be built. The car doesn't pretend to be refined and there are no hi-tech systems – it is built for speed.

The S7R racing version has been extremely successful, winning races all round the world. The original S7 road car had a normally aspirated engine based on a modified Ford V8, similar to the one used in NASCARs. The S7 Twin Turbo appeared in 2005, with twin turbochargers and other engine modifications giving an impressive 750bhp (559kW). In 2006, a 'Competition' package was introduced that included a range of modifications, including improved aerodynamics, suspension and an even more powerful engine giving 1,000bhp (746kW). In 2017, Saleen unveiled the S7 Le Mans (LM) to celebrate its success with the racing version of the S7. This limited edition was priced at $1 million, and had an uprated 7.0-litre twin-turbo engine producing 1,300bhp (969kW)!

# STATISTICS SALEEN S7 TWIN TURBO

| | |
|---|---|
| **Price (new)** | Around £433,000 |
| **Max speed** | 248mph (399kph) |
| **0–60mph (0–97kph)** | 2.8s |
| **Engine type** | Twin-turbo 16-valve V8 |
| **Engine capacity** | 7.0 litres |
| **Max power** | 750bhp (559kW) at 6,300rpm |
| **Max torque** | 949Nm (700lb ft) at 4,800rpm |
| **Transmission** | 6-speed manual gearbox, limited-slip differential |
| **Suspension** | Double wishbones and spring/damper units front and rear |
| **Wheels and tyres** | 19in front wheels; 20in rear wheels; 275/35 R19 front tyres; 335/30 R20 rear tyres |
| **Kerb weight** | 1,346kg |
| **Length** | 4,774mm |
| **Width** | 1,990mm |
| **Height** | 1,041mm |
| **Year introduced** | 2000 |

THE SALEEN COMPANY MADE ITS NAME BUILDING MODIFIED FORD MUSTANGS.

# SSC TUATARA

A stunning American-built hypercar inspired by jet fighter planes

- ➤ The car has so far taken 10 years to develop, and 100 cars will be built.
- ➤ The Tuatara is named after a lizard-like reptile from New Zealand.
- ➤ The car has a digital dash display called a Human-Machine Interface (HMI).
- ➤ The 5.9-litre twin-turbo V8 engine has been built specially for the Tuatura.

The SSC Tuatara is the follow-up to the company's Ultimate Aero, and is designed to try and beat a maximum speed of 300mph (483kph)! The car has extremely good aerodynamics, with a computer-controlled active rear wing that automatically adjusts to give maximum downforce, and acts as an airbrake when the car is braking. The twin-turbo V8 is tuned to produce 1,750bhp (1,305kW)!

SSC (Shelby Super Cars) is an American company that produced the SSC Ultimate Aero in 2007, which was briefly the world's fastest production car (256.18mph/412.28kph), beating the Bugatti Veyron's record. The first production Tuatara is due before the end of 2019. Three suspension modes are provided – 'Sport' for road driving, 'Track' for maximum performance, and 'Front Lift', which raises the suspension for speed bumps, or driving the car on to a ferry! The car's equipment includes air conditioning, digital driver display, touch-screen control system, side cameras for blind-spot vision, rear view camera for reversing, and a premium in-car entertainment system.

# STATISTICS SSC TUATARA

| | |
|---|---|
| Price (new) | Unknown |
| Max speed | Targeted 300mph (483kph) |
| 0–60mph (0–97kph) | Unknown |
| Engine type | Twin-turbo V8 |
| Engine capacity | 5.9 litres |
| Max power | 1,750bhp (1,305kW) on E85 biofuel; 1,350bhp (1,007kW) on 91-octane fuel |
| Max torque | Unknown |
| Transmission | 7-speed semi-automatic gearbox |
| Suspension | Unknown |
| Wheels and tyres | 20in front and rear wheels; 245/35 R20 front tyres; 345/30 R20 rear tyres |
| Kerb weight | 1,247kg |
| Length | 4,633mm |
| Width | 2,065mm |
| Height | 1,067mm |
| Year introduced | 2019 |

THE CAR'S 'BUBBLE-CANOPY' COCKPIT IS INSPIRED BY JET FIGHTER DESIGN.

# TESLA ROADSTER

An electric roadster that could be a look into the future for extreme cars

- ➤ Would-be owners can pre-order a car for a £38,000 deposit.
- ➤ A lightweight removable glass roof panel can be stored in the boot.
- ➤ Tesla aims for the car to be the quickest-accelerating and fastest road car available.
- ➤ The car should have a range of 620 miles (998km) before it needs recharging.

The original Tesla Roadster was built between 2008 and 2012, but the new Roadster that should be delivered to its first owners in 2020 is a completely new car. The Roadster is an all-electric four-seater (though the back seats are very small) and could be the fastest-accelerating road car ever!

The new Roadster had a surprise unveiling in November 2017 during the launch of a future Tesla truck (the Tesla Semi), when a prototype Roadster was driven out of the back of a Semi trailer. The Roadster will be a normal production car instead of a limited-edition hypercar. The first 1,000 cars will be special 'Founder's Series' cars, and anyone who wants to buy one has to pay the full price of £189,000 up front. The car has three electric motors – one at the front and two at the rear to give four-wheel-drive. A 'SpaceX package' will include cold-air thrusters, like the SpaceX spacecraft, to improve cornering and acceleration. The Roadster could change the future for hypercars.

# STATISTICS TESLA ROADSTER

| | |
|---|---|
| Price (new) | Base model around £151,000 |
| Max speed | Claimed 250mph+ (402kph+) |
| 0–60mph (0–97kph) | Claimed 1.9s |
| Engine type | Three electric motors |
| Engine capacity | Not applicable |
| Max power | Unknown |
| Max torque | Wheel torque – 10,000Nm (7,376lb ft) |
| Transmission | Four-wheel drive |
| Suspension | Unknown |
| Wheels and tyres | Unknown |
| Kerb weight | Unknown |
| Length | Unknown |
| Width | Unknown |
| Height | Unknown |
| Year introduced | 2020 |

A 'YOKE'-TYPE STEERING WHEEL IS FITTED, LIKE THE CONTROL COLUMN ON A PLANE.

# ULTIMA RS

A 'build-it-yourself' Le Mans-style car with incredible performance

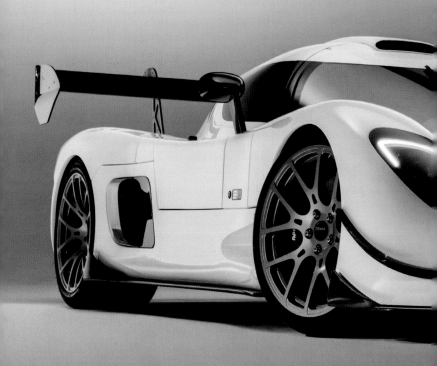

- Options include a rear view camera and parking sensors.
- The RS can brake from 100mph (160kph) to a standstill in an amazing 3.3s!
- Two Ultimas were used as development cars for the McLaren F1 road car.
- For a race-car-like driving experience, no ABS or traction control is fitted.

The British-built Ultima RS was announced in June 2019, and is the fastest and most advanced Ultima so far. It is powered by a Chevrolet V8 engine, and is available with several different power outputs, from a 'basic' 480bhp (358kW), to an incredible 1,200bhp (895kW) for the top-of-the-range supercharged version!

The very first Ultima Mk1 was built in 1983, and was a mid-engined kit-car designed to look like a Le Mans car. It used donor parts from other cars, including Ford and Renault suspension, steering and brake parts, and a Renault engine and gearbox. Since that first car, Ultimas have been constantly updated, and improved, and the company now makes all its own components, apart from the engine and gearbox. The most powerful version of the RS is a genuine hypercar, and is capable of stunning performance with its 1,200bhp (895kW) Chevrolet V8. The RS has air conditioning, in-car entertainment, a digital dashboard with data logging, and an Ultima RS-branded set of luggage, plus an optional kit to lift the front suspension for speed bumps!

# STATISTICS ULTIMA RS

| | |
|---|---|
| **Price (new)** | Around £95,000 |
| **Max speed** | 250mph+ (402kph+) |
| **0–60mph (0–97kph)** | 2.3s |
| **Engine type** | Supercharged Chevrolet V8 |
| **Engine capacity** | 6.2 litres |
| **Max power** | 1,200bhp (895kW) |
| **Max torque** | Unknown |
| **Transmission** | Porsche 6-speed manual |
| **Suspension** | Double wishbones front and rear with coil spring/damper units |
| **Wheels and tyres** | 19in front and rear wheels; 265/30 R19 front tyres; 325/30 R19 rear tyres |
| **Kerb weight** | 930kg |
| **Length** | 4,170mm |
| **Width** | 1,900mm |
| **Height** | 1,125mm |
| **Year introduced** | 2019 |

CARS CAN BE ORDERED FOR SELF-ASSEMBLY, OR FULLY BUILT BY THE FACTORY.

# W MOTORS FENYR SUPERSPORT

## This a wolf-like Supersport looks like it comes from a sci-fi movie

- ➤ Three separate active rear wing flaps are fitted, which move automatically.
- ➤ A second instrument panel is fitted for the passenger to show speed, rpm, etc.
- ➤ The W Motors Fenyr Supersport's doors open rearwards.
- ➤ The body is made from carbon-fibre and graphene composite.

**W** Motors is a design company based in Dubai – the first hypercar designer in the Middle East. The 'W' in W Motors stands for Wolf, and the Fenyr Supersport was named after a ferocious Wolf from Norse mythology. With its astonishing looks, when Batman needs a new Batmobile, this could be the car!

W Motors was founded in 2012, and the Fenyr Supersport is its second hypercar, following on from the Lykan Hypersport, also named after a mythical wolf. Only seven Lykan Hypersports were built, and each car had 440 diamonds in the headlights, and a holographic display in the cockpit! The Fenyr Supersport first appeared in 2017, and each car is hand-built in Italy. The car is powered by a 3.8-litre twin-turbo flat-6 engine, built by specialist tuning company RUF, and based on a Porsche engine. The first 10 cars built will be 'Launch Editions', each one finished in a different unique colour scheme featuring bare carbon-fibre. Only 100 cars will be built after the Launch Editions.

# STATISTICS W MOTORS FENYR SUPERSPORT

| | |
|---|---|
| **Price (new)** | £1.4 million |
| **Max speed** | 248mph (400kph) |
| **0–62mph (0–100kph)** | 2.8s |
| **Engine type** | Porsche-based twin-turbo flat-6 |
| **Engine capacity** | 3,800cc |
| **Max power** | 800bhp (596kW) at 7,100rpm |
| **Max torque** | 980Nm (723lb ft) at 4,000rpm |
| **Transmission** | 7-speed Porsche dual-clutch PDK gearbox, limited-slip differential |
| **Suspension** | Front McPherson struts, rear pushrod-actuated multi-link with horizontal spring/damper units |
| **Wheels and tyres** | 19in front wheels; 20in rear wheels; 265/35 R19 front tyres; 345/30 R20 rear tyres |
| **Kerb weight** | 1,350kg |
| **Length** | 4,600mm |
| **Width** | 1,926mm |
| **Height** | 1,540mm |
| **Year introduced** | 2017 |

STANDARD EQUIPMENT INCLUDES A REAR VIEW CAMERA AND AN INTERNET ROUTER!

# ZENVO TSR-S

A rare, hand-built car from Denmark with a crazy tilting rear wing

- Zenvo builds only five cars each year, and every car is bespoke for its owner.
- A built-in hydraulic system can lift the car up 50mm for extra ground clearance.
- The car has a lightweight steel and aluminium chassis and carbon bodywork.
- The gearbox has a 'Race' mode for lightning-fast gear changes on the track.

The sensational Zenvo TSR-S first appeared at the Geneva Motor Show in 2018. The car has a unique 'Zentripetal' rear wing that moves in two directions. It rotates to act as an airbrake, but it also tilts from side to side when the car is cornering, so the edge of the wing on the outside of the corner is lower than the inside edge!

Zenvo is a Danish hypercar company that was founded in 2004, and built its first car in 2009. The company designs and builds its own engines, but so far has only built 25 cars. The TSR-S (the 'S' stands for 'street') was developed from the TSR track car, and is designed to be equally at home on the track or on the road. The car has three driving modes – 'Minimum' (700bhp/522kW), 'IQ' and 'Maximum' (1,177bhp/878kW). The IQ setting automatically controls the maximum power depending on the conditions. Options such as air conditioning, satnav, air bags and a sound system can be fitted for no extra cost.

# STATISTICS ZENVO TSR-S

| | |
|---|---|
| **Price (new)** | More than £1.3 million |
| **Max speed** | 202mph (325kph) |
| **0–62mph (0–100kph)** | 2.8s |
| **Engine type** | Twin-supercharged V8 |
| **Engine capacity** | 5.8 litres |
| **Max power** | 1,177bhp (878kW) at 8,500rpm |
| **Max torque** | 1,100Nm (811lb ft) |
| **Transmission** | 7-speed paddle-shift gearbox, limited-slip differential |
| **Suspension** | Double wishbones front and rear |
| **Wheels and tyres** | 20in front wheels; 21in rear wheels; 245/35 R20 front tyres; 325/30R21 rear tyres |
| **Kerb weight** | 1,495kg |
| **Length** | 4,815mm |
| **Width** | 2,038mm |
| **Height** | 1,198mm |
| **Year introduced** | 2018 |

OWNERS CAN HAVE A CUSTOM 'WATERMARK' INCLUDED UNDER THE CAR'S GLOSS FINISH.